VITAL SIGNS

VITAL SIGNS

Poetry by Juan Delgado

Photography by Thomas McGovern

Heyday, Berkeley, California
Inlandia Institute, Riverside, California

This Inlandia book was published by Heyday and Inlandia Institute.

Poetry © 2013 by Juan Delgado
Photography © 2013 by Thomas McGovern

Library of Congress Cataloging-in-Publication Data
Delgado, Juan, 1960-
 [Poems. Selections]
 Vital signs / poetry by Juan Delgado ; photography by Thomas McGovern.
    pages cm
 Photos by Thomas McGovern of hand-made signs and murals throughout California's Inland
Empire, poems by Juan Delgado. The book will preserve the narrative and visual culture of the
area, which is under threat by urban renewal and development.
 ISBN 978-1-59714-250-2 (pbk. : alk. paper)
 1. Inland Empire (Calif.)--Poetry. 2. Inland Empire (Calif.)--Pictorial works. I. McGovern,
Thomas, 1957- illustrator. II. Title.
 PS3554.E442465V58 2013
 811'.54--dc23
                              2013000264

Cover Art: Thomas McGovern
Cover Design: Lorraine Rath
Interior Design/Typesetting: Rebecca LeGates

Orders, inquiries, and correspondence should be addressed to:
        Heyday
        P.O. Box 9145, Berkeley, CA 94709
        (510) 549-3564, Fax (510) 549-1889
        www.heydaybooks.com

Manufactured by Regent Publishing Services, China

10 9 8 7 6 5 4 3 2 1

Contents

VITAL SIGNS

A Point West of Mount San Bernardino

For Father Bob

I.

> By the road she hovers in heat waves,
> propped up on a cinderblock wall,
> revived by mixed house paints,
> fending for herself like wild mint.

She is behind your shoulder,
a blind spot, your city's poverty.
A figure waits under a freeway ramp,
gesturing as if she knows you.

> The fences and lots have the same dogs,
> peering through the chain-links, curious.

While at the hospital, you see kids play another
game of tag outside the emergency room doors
and know how fingerprints squander their ridges
and how digital minutes dry up under a glare.

II.

A stump is all that is left of a surveyor's point,
a ponderosa pine in the foothills that started
the city's perfect grid.
                              The sidewalks of Baseline
need more than a grocery bag's empty belly,
plastic, a ripped-up flame standing and calling
out to an old preacher like yourself.
                                    By the cameras
mounted on the street lights, you wonder
if they recorded the street sinking in the eyes
of the woman who died on a bus bench.

You pause in front of a freshly painted sign
that says "Wrong Way," and see a sign within
a sign, a resistance to the newest strip mall,
the black lettering unevenly spaced and painted,
a homespun warning to keep moving on.

Crown after Crown

For Ernest

Goatheads bask in their thorns
        and roar on spoked wheels,
sun-burnt, falling to the roadside
        and spreading their seeds.

We, too, cling to our poor
            soil-rooted dreams,
the return of our lands. St. Augustine
will not smother us again.
        We have our crown of thistles.

We are a prong-stubborn people,
        dirty cheeked, and in spring
the lemon-yellow flowers
        of our goatheads bloom.

Lavish Weeds

I. The Hula Dancer with More Than One Biography

For Larry

Let's gather to see his bronze lamp dance;
she wiggles her grass skirt under a shade.
She was never a throwaway, though unnoticed,
waiting for a buyer under her burnt-out moon.

"In the end, how alike are we to her?" he asks.
"We don't outlive our clothing; someone else
will point to the tarnished jewelry of our wives
or peer through glass at cuff links that were ours."

I know a man who collects pipes, tar-throated
and plugged up beyond repair, and lays them
at the feet of a Hawaiian dancer who gleams,
like the Brown Virgin, her ever-reaching arms
wanting you to surrender to her constancy, her beauty.

II. You Kept Surfacing, Reeling Yellow

In my backyard, we were casting,
our pond the shade of an orange tree.
The weight flew, bouncing on the grass
and fallen blossoms, yellowing petals.

I recalled their mouths, a postcard
of Guanajuato's mummies, dug up
if their relatives could not pay a tax.
They were brushed off, wired into
a pose for the tourists, still wearing
their Sunday best.
                              "Just relax your wrist,"
you said, teaching me your nylon line,
piss-yellow was less likely to tangle
like a new spool with no
                              history of unraveling.
So, we fished among the rotting orange
peels, avoiding the dog-chewed Frisbee.

A friend had made her peace with you,
your illness, but you were not ready,
still driving to the City of Hope
for treatments.

                         Your brittle bones
had termites, so they kept tenting
and fumigating you.
                    "Just relax,"
you kept saying that day we cast
and reeled in a hookless line blending
into the evening, calm, no ripples
against the hull or splashes
of a surfacing fish or turbulence
of another boat's wake.
                              Still intent,
standing more in the middle of our pond,
you were not done with my lesson.

III. You Touch Red, Red Touches You

In his Spanish balcony his wrists get thinner,
the stems of a rosemary. He wonders, "Is
         the toll higher when returning
         from the crossing?"

On his shelf, a book observes the light rising
         with the specks of a whisper and listens.
         His turquoise ring, gaudy as a church
         made from beehives, is suspended,   trembling.
         The blood of his spit stains deeper down   into
         a pillow's heart. From his carpet fibers   the dust
         of his footsteps goes airborne;   with choppy breaths
he takes himself in, pauses, and begins again,
a king snake vanishing in and appearing out
of gopher holes.

IV. The Sweet and Bitter Monuments of Clutter

For you, we had a service. In a monastery no less.
Why didn't I stop your mourners?
I lacked the resolve of a jeweler's glass eye—
you had earned a service at Valley Thrift,
your favorite junk store in San Bernardino.

In a casket of trunks held by silver duct-tape,
I should've wheeled you past the racks of the faded
and wrinkled clothing, leaving us wondering
when we spotted our favorite outfit hanging there
whether we should be buried with our beloved objects.

Growing up in the absence of a mother's sanity
and hearing her daily sermons, you preferred
the fragments of a religion, the rebirth
of the discarded, so among the incomplete
bedroom set and the sagging cushions of a sofa,
I should've left you, saying you had had an untidy life,
rattled by the aftershocks of a divorce and held up
by the steady legs of a merry-go-round table
you bothered to restore one rainy weekend.

V. While the Brown-headed Cowbirds Migrate

The Santa Ana River flashed
in the lines of your palm. You drank.
Composed as a river's tongue,
          you walked in hip-high grasses
while the dragonflies hovered near
your right shoulder blade,
an unsettled buzzing.

          While the verdolagas rooted down,
populating the cracks of our parking lots,
you saw the faceless bubble gum spots
in front of the wide doors of our police station
harden under the weight of our city.

You lingered with the San Berdoo whores,
the shoulder leaners of cinderblock walls,
the beauty queens of our Party Doll Lounge,
generous as any Midwest farmer
with his bounty.

              Their grotesquely large
         hands eased your pitted face,
your troubles. Like the old masters,
         you forged your own cross,
letting its body hiss, a rage
dissolving in water, holding it
         long enough until it burned,
drying the sweat of your palm.

You left poems, thick-coated,
varnished, flaking yellow,
         still breathing and expanding,
the knots of a pine
ceiling, brown eyes, not
         so common to us now.

Como Llora el Viento

I. Lo Desconocido (The Unknown)

You are bound up by your own bones.
Who knew you were coming, Gloria?
While another hand pats your son's
shoulder, bringing no news to his ear,
the desert sweeps over your tennis shoe,
its sole facing the desert sun. Did you
know what to pack for such a journey?

In a country of guarded borders that funnel
people into a mouth of blistering heat
and of recliners that drift into a TV glow,
you are not a news chime starting the hour,
but a backpack's strap, matches from Nogales,
cortisone cream, and the half star of a ring,
scattered under the shade of a creosote bush.

II. Southern California Bound

Making it further than you, your son sits
on top of a Union Pacific train, holding on
and flying into a heavy fog. The pounding
of wheels is a warning of what is to come.

The graffiti recites with a freight yard's haste.

Gloria, you are a worn-out photo, tucked into
his front pocket, tapped often like a memory.
Once the fog settles, he sees a willow tree
lose its trunk in the murk, rootless like you.

Needing a funeral, wind-tousled, tumble-
weed roaming, how will he recognize you?

The faucets of your farm are hunched over,
and the splinters in your son's palms burn,
pointing to el Norte like your village's crosses.

For Jorge

You appear wearing your only white shirt,
weighing the perfect dirt clod in your hand,
ready to dash off to the nearest field of foxtails.
Why did mother always call my name first
when she wanted you to get going to school?
How many times did I have to wash your face?
And what a fuss you were on Sunday mornings.
Once you came to me, clenching your hand,
raising your fist. "Look," you said, "My palm
is on fire, ant bites!" You had carried a clod
across the field and through our alley, finding
the perfect wall for exploding your grenade.
Next time, I'll run cool water over the burning
and wake the whole house to your pain, I promise.

Tona

My wife didn't bathe in a stream to keep
the fetus in the right position. And I
didn't cut our dog's leash to ensure
the umbilical cord would not strangle
our son.

         At the swap meet a stroller held
a plastic baby facing a maze of stalls.
Its glass eyes never blinked in the sun.
A clothesline hanging over the baby held
a white coat on a hanger; it was tiny,
a baptism suit. Its coat pockets were
sewn shut.

              Mother, don't blame us now
that our son is so sick for not using
the nickname you gave us, so no one
could harm him by using his real name.

The Evidence Is Everywhere

I.

The Santa Anas, childlike and profound,
blanket me; I see the dust stirring the valley
and clouding downtown San Bernardino;
I feel the sting of your loss.

The black oak leaves, brittle, tumbling,
crack under my feet. Is your hand
touching the dryness of my lips?

You sing: "Don't sit, mountain-still,
a coyote skull whistling."

I tug at the skin on my wrist, trying
to peel off the seam, my stubbornness.

On Sunday, I wear my only
decent dress, gypsy-green.
I hear heels scurry around me.
Our priest is a hinged tongue,
his verse tucking us in.

Why can't I focus on anyone's face?

II.

The winds fly from a canyon's belly
into a peasant blouse.

A stampede of leaves and twigs rushes by
a patch of grass, scraping across a sidewalk
and dragging their nails, fierce and defiant
as a local poet's words.

From the sides of mountains, waterfalls
of dust form, and during my pilgrimage,
the fate of lip-stained Styrofoam cups
will not unnerve me. Not worried
about compasses, I'll go by fences guarding
abandoned lots, through desperate patches of grass,
yellowing, past one-legged billboards of paper
and glue. Resting under the shade of bus stops,
I'll recite old tales to ward off the haunted
and the debris of family floods piling up.

When the voices on an updraft emphatically
circle like red-tailed hawks, I'll recall
the tail of a comet urging you to wrap
yourself in its flames and dissolve.
Entranced by a burning equal to yours,
I'll walk eighty miles, traveling the routes
of my childhood candy wrappers.

III.

In the moisture
of a dirt road I traveled,
you are the rain that visited
the night before.

Does your tongue sense
the heat of bodies flying
in the Santa Anas?

Again, I am lost tracing
your face, a dry playa,
the eyes of clay, a brown
maze of upward glances.

Are you a creek bridge,
a fallen cedar, lodged
between sunbaked boulders
inviting me to cross?

You are the one
taking away my fear
of being wheeled down
a hallway without doors.

IV.

With twigs in my hair, I was found
somewhere near the national forest.
Bystanders pulled back their sniffing dogs
while I stood, barefoot and tired.

When I predicted earthquakes in China,
Peru and Cucamonga, California,
I baffled my psychiatric ward.

After a nurse removed my handout
of *The Seasons: Winter,* wildlife appeared
on the hospital grounds. A mule deer's
antlers surfaced in the parking lot,
weaving among the staff's cars.
A coyote leaped into the patients' garden
and howled under a security light
as if to say: "I am here. Where are you?"
A roadrunner scooted across a lot,
losing one of its long tail feathers.
All this had the staff checking again
if their office windows were latched.

In my notebook, I drew a coy face
with blurry dots for eyes that peer out
of a hollow trunk, struck by lightning,
charred by fire, with smoke still rising
under your vaulted sky.

V.

Outside my window,
      the sky is suddenly
draped by a hum,
      a hummingbird's hunger.
Her wings wrinkle the sky.
            Unlike
a chickadee too busy
and full of seed chatter,
      the hummingbird
puffs up the air,
feeding like a storm,
a redness, a sideway rocket
      past the world's ear.

That spark reminds me of you.

Thin-rooted, lingering too
long, absorbed in window
reveries, I'll be released. Here,
the soil is moist, sponge-like,
storing. Worms surface,
      digesting their way up.
I, too, am ready
for the driving winds
      of another season.

Vecinos

The viejitas of our calle
guard our niños and barrio
like the santos that line
their windowsills at night.
As their prayers flicker,
they take comfort
in their plastic rosaries.

The viejitas of our calle
taste the cilantro and yerbabuena
of their childhood jardines
and smell like the wooden
pews of our corner iglesias.
Unlike us, they are not
scared about living aquí.

The viejitas of our calle
spit out the thorns of their past.
Not given to laziness
like their jefes, they stitch
and patch new familias together,
these viejitas, wind-driven
beyond their own raíces.

Just Enough   of That

I.

Above, a red-tailed hawk freewheels, southbound;
a palm tree laments the heat; its shadow is on time.
A faucet drips, a moss tear down the pipe's neck.
Smog taints her trailer's windows, and the Santa Anas'
dust streaks sparkle.   The forklift air leaves a rusty taste.

        With patches of yellow, the crabgrass undercuts her efforts,
        her lawn fenced in and crowned by barbed wire.

She is in purple loose-fitting sweats, overdue by
a week, and rakes away dirt clods with her hand,
then hurriedly pats the dirt mound, a foot-stomping,
a sad dance   "Deep enough. Coyotes can only sniff."

        A butterfly bounces by: "Must look, must look again
        for the extra key. He's almost here. Hours away.
        His poor doggy, poor Max. Bobby arrives today."

II.

Her driveway is no longer a dash to the gate, teeth
glaring beyond the links at a passing neighbor's   dog.
She, too, is tossed up, and the drought in her head
goes beyond the freeway's crawling pillars, shadows
so much like people, so much like her clock's hands
moving until they stand still without their shadows
            leaning away from them, their other selves   gone,
the ones they are used to locating, recurring   memories.

Tangled up,   a frantic hand brushing poetic,
she is   a fence tearing up Safeway bags in a wind chant.
                 She walks: "Where's his water bowl? Sit Bobby
down,   give him tags. Must find the water bowl first.
                      Key on nail, hanging behind door." With hands
clutching   up her belly, she stops, "Oh no, not now."

Peculiar Properties

On my cutting board, I discovered them,
the tiniest of ants, roaming dots of lead.
At first, they were too few to classify, hiding
under crumbs, these scavengers of leftovers.
Admiring their labor, I immediately granted them
citizenship, these tailgaters of a kitchen's routines.

In Miami, I had no stove, working far from my home.
My wife was a midnight call to San Bernardino.
While searching for crumbs, especially for
the taste of apricot jelly, they fell into a line
across my cutting board; I saw it again,
saw the line my sixth-grade teacher drew
on the board, pointing to each end.

While he planted himself on his desk, he leaned
his face toward us, telling us in a low voice:

"You don't see it yet, you're too young
still, but that line in front of you continues
infinitely on either side. And if there is
the slightest slope in that line, either way,
it will slowly begin to sag, then curve and veer
and eventually one end will find the other.

And lines, lines are never perfect, they are
like us, never completely straight. So just
imagine the searching that goes on all
around us, every day. And to happen on
that union is really to witness the most earthly
of forms you'll ever get to know. If you're lucky,
you'll see that, even luckier if you're part
of that union."

Skipping

For Anna and Clara

He saw the world fetch his daughters a rope.
The dust of their chalk drawings on the sidewalk
jumped in while their ponytails loosened.

       On a staircase dulled by a weak light,
       they would stop in midstep and giggle
       for no obvious reason before vanishing.

Their whole street slid off the refrigerator's magnet.
Like stars at dawn, their peanut butter fingerprints
receded into a Whirlpool's black door.

Often he walked to the yard's edge far enough
to where he could see them make their unsteady
turns on their Stingrays, spotting the dead
crabgrass rising from their spokes like sparks.

       They squinted between their handlebars
       and pumped their pedals faster, flying back
       with the ruckus of hungry jays at dusk.

Marshall Street: Standing Water

On our way, a crow in the sprinkler-
soaked ivy sinks deeper until we can
hear it squawk only when we pass,
the ivy's leaves trembling in sunlight.

Later, we notice on the roadside, wings,
spread out in flight, headless, and glued
to the asphalt by their dried blood.

We hurry the kids along when they ask
"What's wrong?" We hurry them past
the fallen birds and the ones suddenly
appearing in the middle of our yard.

We begin to study the pools of water,
the still water, the untreated water,
turning green in our sleep, breeding:

a hand that nudges us beyond the unusual;
a pair of eyes that can gaze only inward;
a beak that sings into its own ruffled chest.

Crates

In early May, we had one last winter storm—
the snow fell in clusters from the oak branches,
drooping, sun-heavy, dripping like rain gutters.
The bear-bark cedars believed, like me,
the drought would soon be over. Eagerly,
I shoveled my driveway, new to berms.

A Saturday morning I was caught up
watching the ladybugs with their spotted
shells punctuating the air; they floated over
the creek's coolness. I, too, drifted through
my yard, picking up my recently bought rake.
With enough good soil for my irises to take,
I dug, wondering about the ash pile
I came upon. Where did the ashes come from?
A fireplace? Did the previous owner dump
and spread them among my pines and newly
framed-in flower bed? I was so far away
from the sidewalks and lots covered by darkened
bubble gum spots, the overturned grocery carts,
and the flaking ads of sun-burnt billboards.

In June, monarch butterflies fed on daisies,
showy milkweed, and black-eyed Susans,
preferring their fragrances. They glided through,
erratic, bouncing in their air trails and seemingly
stitching my mountain range to the valley below.
That first summer, I planted more irises,
kicking up the dust of another owner's fires,
studying the bark beetles' droppings embedded
in the sap, the glittering mouth-shaped wound
of my sugar pine. I touched the sap with my finger,
smelling the sweet scent that was quickly covered
over by ash when I patted the soil down.

On a late morning in October, I saw
from our canyon road the smoke appearing
distant at first, but quickly the ash covered
my car's windshield. I asked myself,
"Which road will close first? Who will free
my neighbor's restless cats? What good are hoses
when the flames funnel up the ridges of canyons
and leap across highways?" To think more deeply
would terrify me, and though my house was
not in imminent danger, I drove back home,
rushing to my front door, jamming the key in,
unable to turn the lock. "Which neighbor is home?"
I considered what I should pack, trying to assure
myself I had received more than I owned.

I stacked boxes of photos on my kitchen counter,
spotting the screen door of my childhood home,
drab, not yet boarded up by plywood planks.
When was the last time I thought of that girl?
I glanced at my pine-lined walls, my floors,
everything was made of wood, and I felt
like running again. I was back in Rialto,
making my way through the market's alley
where the trash bins bred fruit flies that hovered
among the tossed-away produce boxes.
I saw the owner's son smashing tomato crates.
His boots stomped the wire-bound slats,
snapping them like ribs. He turned, saying,
"Hey! What the fuck are you looking at?"

I ran down the alley without looking back,
running toward another man, who wore
an oversized, dirty sweatshirt, its collar
ringed with sweat stains. "Puro Indio,"
my mother would have uttered. He pushed
a wooden crate, the ones used to ship oranges,
lemons, and grapefruit on the beds of semi trucks.
He had mounted wheels on his large crate,
the kind of wheels found on grocery carts.
"How clever," I thought back then. The wheels
squeaked over the asphalt cracks. Back-bent,
looking beyond me, he steered, veering to avoid
potholes. I pressed my back against a wall,
letting him pass. That's when I saw her.

There inside the crate, a girl my age slept.
A loaf of bread trembled beside her, and a jar
of water glistened by her bare feet. She wore
a blue blouse like the girl at Irene's Market.
I heard the shrill of a wheel stuck in a rut;
the loaf jumped and butted against her.
I felt like reaching into the crate and waking her.
Why hadn't she opened her eyes? I ran again,
my feet taking me back to the wishing well,
one of our town's landmarks, its bricks not yet
chipped and whitewashed, its mouth not yet
cemented in. As kids, we peered in, tip-toed,
watching the water distort and magnify the faces
of coins, all out of reach behind a rebar grid.

Later, I rehearsed what I would tell my parents.
Why was I in the alley? What was I meant to do?
Have I been running away from her ever since?

Deep in the Back Woods of Him

His tutored and idled
tongues strolled,
pinching off a fact
and spitting it out,
an empty seed.

His art had no belly
for an all-too-common
truth, the man standing
beside his own life,
a flagpole waiting
for a special day.

His tongues, dark
as cheap ink, feasted
until they couldn't
wiggle out words
from a circling net.

He rested on the mud
of his dreams, comfy,
hearing the rain gossip.

Fathers and Sons at Barbershops

While a barbershop's candy cane spins, a boy waits.
His father nudges him inside where the barber's foot
stomps, pumping a pedal that lifts a chair. Another boy
is draped, trying not to cry, his first haircut.

A third boy is waiting next to his stepfather,
their elbows touch as they flip through magazines.
The smoke of a cigarette lingers near his shoulders,
then vanishes above the Saturday headlines.

Some sons never return their fathers' glances,
others hide their fists behind the barber's sheet,
their jaws locked; another boy feels the ache
when the barber's hand steers his head into place
and pushes his chin down into his chest;
he blows into the boy's ear, digging his finger in.

The boys are free when their collars are undone;
the sheets are shaken free of hair. They jump off,
brushing off the smell of baby powder from their noses.

One boy will repeatedly think the hand holding his
is strangely not his father's when they leave and cross
the street that usually leads him to his mother's house.

Eva and Howard

For Jorge Teillier

I.

His plans to fix the generator's throttle
are hers now, though their chores are
mapped out on their rug's worn paths.
Howard would speak into his teacup.
The newspaper would lie on his lap
until he had finished his breakfast.
Eva would be mad at him until noon
for leaving it disheveled on her counter.

She decides to wear the sweater he gave her,
its sleeves mended more than once,
frayed, her humming woven into its wool.

His walking stick still takes her outside;
Drawknife shaped, its body no longer casts
a bent-knee stride and its hinged shadow.

II.

Her necklace is made of braided shoelaces
holding a house key; she doesn't feel the cold
anymore while walking in the morning's frost,
hearing a thin layer crackle under her feet.
Eva sees some green apples shaking on
their branches, ice tears clinging to them.
Her mind feeds like a mountain chickadee;
her husband's ax is deep in an oak stump,
and his kindling is scattered around it;
her potbelly stove is no longer a nest for ashes.
She sees her footprints are a way back home,
but gone is the sudden joy of finding a fallen
and aged oak branch for their fireplace stove,
thick enough to burn through their night.

The Singer, Amparo

Draws in faces, children running
after her touring van's back window.
They drift off, heads lowered, hands
on their knees, catching their breath,
seeing her face framed behind
the speeding van's scratched glass.

                    ¿Quién tiene la voz?

The velvet curtains of her ex-lover's
windows were yanked from their clips
and sewn into a dress she carries,
floating through the street, a growing
parade of faces behind her flag.
On a stage she sings barefoot,
offering up her half-naked voice.
In the barrio, pans of grease stop hissing

Manuela

Para Ofelia Camacho Delgado

Se despierta al olor de oveja,
tratando de sacudírselo de las manos.
Luciéndose en sus colores indígenas,
se para al lado de un camión turístico, ella es
una flor de diente de león dorado
como los botones tejidos de su suéter.
Está cansada de los turistas
tomándole su foto, abrazando un cordero.

Sin papeles oficiales en país nuevo
ella camina con brío, y obscenamente despacio,
una lengua extranjera se desliza; sus escamas son
las palabras que ella aun no ha aprendido a confiar.
La pequeñita escondiéndose en el nido de su vientre
hablará quechua primero, *runa*.   "gente"

Los caballos enfermos se echan de
la cubierta del barco con rumbo a Cuba.
Persiguiéndolo, sus cabezas meciéndose,
bufando la sal de sus fosas,
patean. Cuanto más aguanten,
nadarán en las olas hundiéndolos, quedándose
atrás del olor del barco, marranos y hombres.

¿Conoces a alguién que necesite ánimo?
¿Por qué no intentar la fragancia de lavanda o de rosa?

Al fondo del corredor, una máquina suena
y escupe cubitos de hielo, algunos cayéndose,
transparentes sobre las ramas manchadas de la alfombra.
Manuela empuja un carrito de toallas, champú,
loción y jabones perfumados con aceite de rosa.
Fijándose en los letreros de, "No molesten,"
ella pasa por delante del banquero tomándose su tercera ducha
y de la madre dándoles el pecho a sus gemelos en una manta
tendida en el piso. Las mirillas están
silenciosas como un montón de almohadas sucias, algunas oscuras
nunca parpadeando, otras agujeros de luz.
Antes de salir del Day's Inn en la calle Mt. Vernon,
ella se roba unas barras de jabón para su hija
quien las pone en los cajones de su cómoda,
perfumando su ropa interior, tan fresca como flores recien cortadas.

La raíz del diente de león, más profunda,
tolerante a sequías y a tierra mala,
no es una presencia fácilmente desarraigada.

Manuela oye el crujido de las tablas,
el ondear de las velas, los pisoteos de los caballos,
nerviosos, ojeando a la luna llena. Ella ve
las huellas de las pezuñas en la arena, huellas
saliendo del mar y desapareciendo al interior.
Se despierta a ese olor otra vez.

Esta vez ella se para al lado de su ciudad Inca,
sus picos verdes partiendo el cielo,
pintada en la pared del restaurante La Carreta.
Su hija le está tomando su foto,
diciéndole, "Sonríe, Mami, sonríe."

Los caballos con los ojos vendados los cargan izados
en cincho de panza, y sus patas atadas,
ligeramente tocando la cubierta, suspendidos
casi todo el viaje por mar, pero una vez en tierra
algunos escaparán y revertirán a lo salvaje.

¿Conoces a alguién que necesite ánimo?
¿Por qué no intentar la fragancia de lavanda o de rosa?

Ella deja que entre el desierto, salvia silvestre.
El desierto le recuerda a su tierra
mientras el marrano de un granjero cruza la carretera.
Ve que su identificación falsificada vuela del tablero.
Giran las ruedas de su carro volcado:
Suspendida, abrochada a su asiento, pies colgantes,
divisa la luna en los fragmentos del parabrisas,
pozo de lágrimas congeladas,
una mirilla le parpadea a ciegas.

La muerte cae como una pezuña.
Una ráfaga de viento empuja las semillas
del diente de león a lo alto, un rebaño blanco,
un vestido de gasa flotando sobre las yucas.
Su memoria es la fragancia de las barras de jabón
refugiándose en el cajón de su hija.

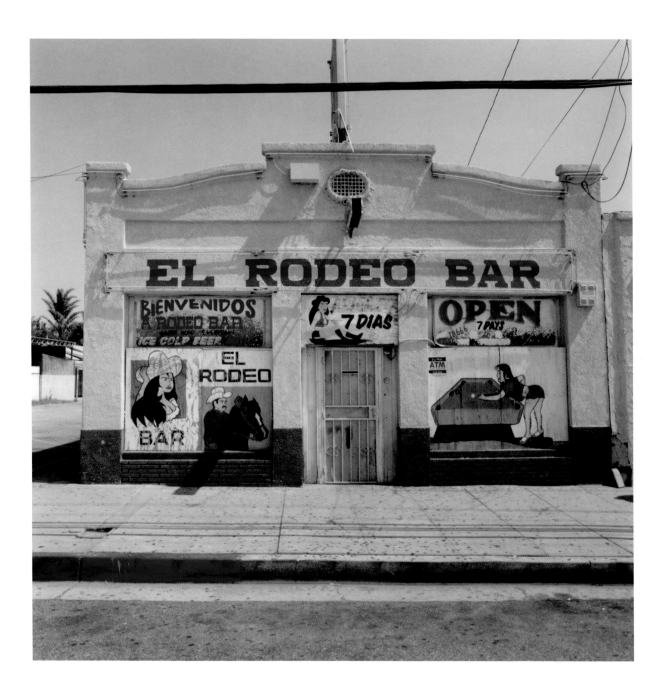

Manuela

For Ofelia Camacho Delgado

She wakes to the odor of sheep,
trying to rub it off her hands.
Dressed up in her native colors,
standing by a tourist van, she is
a dandelion, golden like the alpaca
woven buttons of her sweater.
She is done with the tourists
taking her photo, holding a baby lamb.

Without official papers in a new country,
she briskly walks, and obscenely slow,
a foreign tongue slithers by; its scales are
the words she has not yet learned to trust.
The baby girl hiding in her belly's nest
will learn Quechua first, *runa*.   the people

The sick horses are pushed off
the deck of a ship bound for Cuba.
Pursuing, their heads bobbing,
clearing the salt from their nostrils,
they kick. As long as they can,
they swim in the rushing swells, falling
behind the ship's scent, swine and men.

Know someone who needs their spirits lifted?
Why not try a lavender or a rose scent?

At the end of a hallway, a machine rattles
and spits out ice cubes, some dropping,
transparent on the dull vines of the carpet.
Manuela pushes a cart of towels, shampoo,
lotion, and soap bars scented with rose oil.
Glancing down at the "Do Not Disturb" signs,
she walks past the banker taking his third shower
and the mother nursing her twins on a blanket
spread across the floor. The peepholes are
silent as a pile of dirty pillows, some dark
never blinking, others bullet holes of light.
Before leaving the Day's Inn on Mt. Vernon,
she steals a few soap bars for her daughter,
who places them in her dresser drawers,
scenting her lingerie, fresh as cut flowers.

A dandelion's root, far deeper,
tolerant of drought and poor soil,
is not an easily uprooted presence.

Manuela hears the creaking of planks,
the flapping of sails, and horses stomping,
nervous, eyeing the full moon. She sees
the marks of hooves in the sand, marks
coming out from the sea and vanishing inland.
She wakes to that odor again.

This time she stands beside her Incan city,
its green peaks cutting the sky open,
painted on La Carreta Restaurant's wall.
Her daughter is taking her photo,
saying, *"Sonríe, Mami, sonríe."*   "Smile, Mom, smile."

The blindfolded horses are hoisted on board
in belly slings, and their feet are tied,
slightly touching the deck, suspended
for most of the voyage, but once on land
some will escape and revert to the wild.

Know someone who needs their spirits lifted?
Why not try a lavender or a rose scent?

She lets the desert in, wild sage.
The desert takes her back home
while a farmer's pig crosses the highway.
She sees her fake ID fly off the dashboard.
The wheels of her upside-down car spin:
Suspended, buckled to her seat, feet dangling,
she spots the moon on the shards
of her windshield, frozen tears,
the peepholes blinking back at her.

Death touches down like a hoof.
A gust of wind pushes the seeds
of dandelions upward, a flock of white,
a gauze gown drifting over yuccas.
Memory is the scent of soap bars
taking refuge in a daughter's drawer.

Old and New Fires of San Bernardino

The ash
      filling the mouths of lemon blossoms
smothers a fishpond.

          . . .

      In a morning, what can be carried
      beyond memory?

          . . .

After losing their invisibility, spiderwebs
                              tremble,
the ash beards of walls.

          . . .

                The fire's throat whirls up
a small tornado beside a eucalyptus tree,
      spitting out embers that bounce off walls,
porches, and decks; others fly into window eaves,
worming up against floor studs, and plot.

          . . .

A car on a driveway stacked with boxes chokes a hose
trying to reach a neighbor's frantic curtains.

· · ·

Inside the eucalyptus, its tar-black belly and veins
burn, and out of a branch a flame appears waving.

· · ·

Large plumes bruise the sky;
a row of stucco houses goes to their knees, and doorknobs
lying on the ground point
to past interiors and imagined ones yet to be built,
intimate residences all.

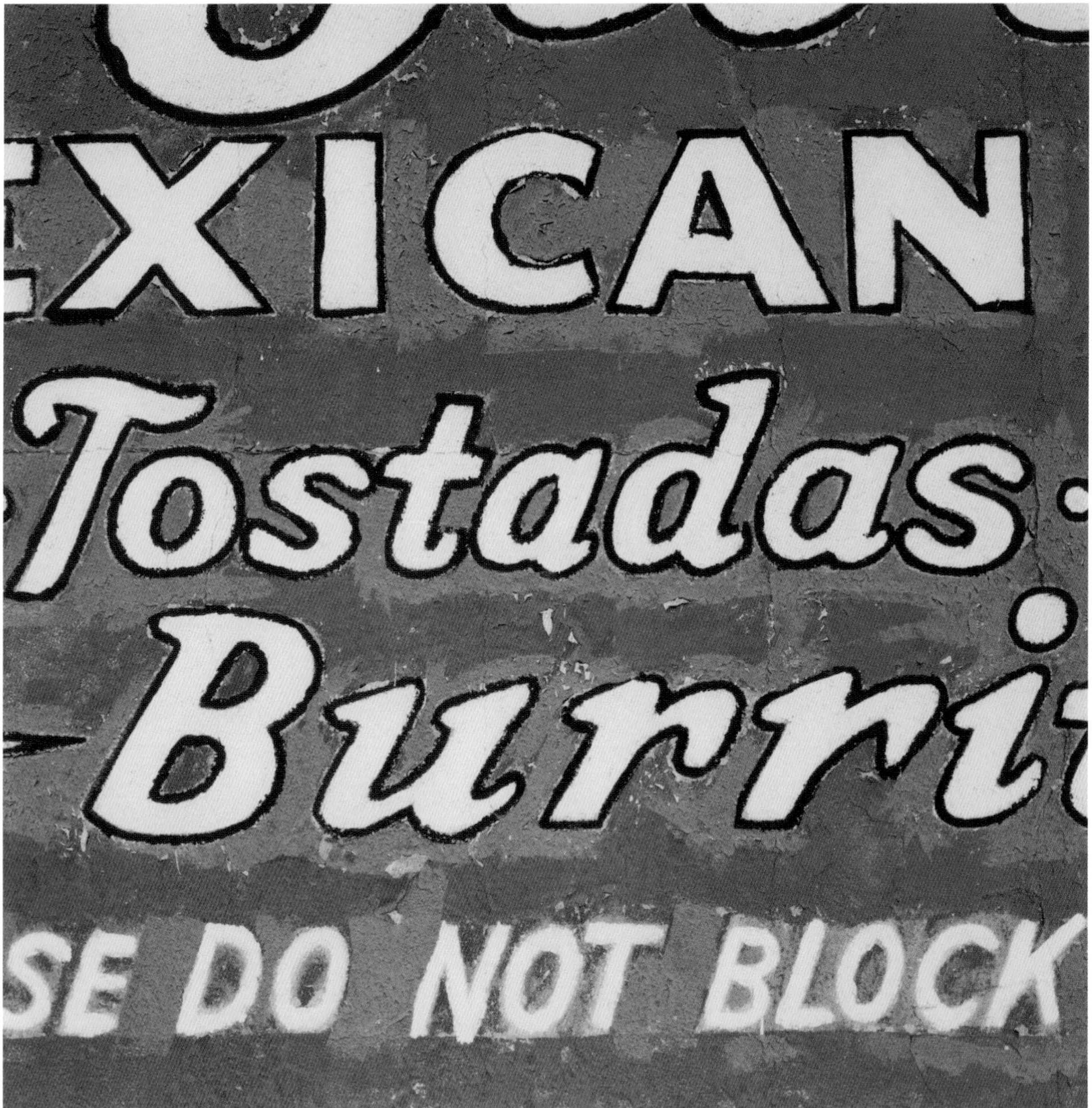
EXICAN
Tostadas
Burri
SE DO NOT BLOCK

Acknowledgments

This book was made possible by generous donations from:
Dr. Albert Karnig, President, California State University, San Bernardino
Dr. Andrew Bodman, Provost, California State University, San Bernardino
Dr. Eri Yasuhara, Dean, College of Arts and Letters, California State University, San Bernardino
Pamela Langford, Director, Alumni Affairs, California State University, San Bernardino

Additional financial support for this book was provided by Karen Eastman. Financial support for the creation of some of this work was provided through Professional Development Grants and Summer Fellowships from California State University, San Bernardino.

Many people provided support and encouragement and deserve my thanks, including Andi Campognone, curator of the Lancaster Museum of Art and History; Daniel Foster, executive director of the Community Foundation; Marion Mitchell-Wilson, director of the Inlandia Institute; Rebecca Trawick, curator of the Wignall Museum of Contemporary Art; Jessica Wyland, founder of the Wild Lemon Project; and friends Don Solarzano and Don Woodford. Special thanks to my dear friend Louis Fox, who suggested this photography project. The photographs would not have been possible without the constant guidance, criticism, and support of my beloved wife, Renate.

—Thomas McGovern

I am extremely grateful to Julie Paegle, Steve Lehigh, Maria Notarangelo, and Antonieta Gallegos-Ruiz for their support and thoughtful suggestions and feedback. Special thanks go to my sister, Ofelia Fitzpatrick, for her Spanish translation of "Manuela." As always, I want to express my love for Jean, my wife for thirty years. Lastly, Clara, Marco, and Anna, you're the best kids a dad could have.

I want to note that Section V of "The Evidence Is Everywhere" appeared in *Aperçus Quarterly* 1.3. "Wood Stilts" and "El Tigre Market" appeared in *Bear Flag Republic* (Greenhouse Review Press, 2008): 149–151. Versions of "Old and New Fires of San Bernardino," "Peculiar Properties," and "The Singer, Amparo" appeared in *Hubbub* Vol. 21 (2005): 21–23. A version of "You Kept Surfacing, Reeling Yellow" appeared in *Faultline* (2005): 36. "A Point West of Mount San Bernardino" and "Vecinos" will appear in *Street Lit*, forthcoming from Scarecrow Press.

—Juan Delgado

About the Photographer

Thomas McGovern is a photographer, writer, and educator, and the author of *Bearing Witness (to AIDS)* (1999, Visual AIDS/A.R.T. Press); *Amazing Grace* (2010, Parker Publishing), and *Hard Boys + Bad Girls* (2010, Schiffer Books). His photographs are in the permanent collections of The Museum of Fine Arts, Houston; The Brooklyn Museum; The Baltimore Museum of Art; The Museum of the City of New York; and the New York Historical Society, among others. His art reviews and features have appeared in *Afterimage*, *Artweek*, *Art Issues*, and *Art Papers* and in 2011 he founded the photography publication *Dotphotozine*. He is a professor of art at California State University, San Bernardino.

About the Poet

Juan Delgado has published two chapbooks, *Working on It* and *A Change of Worlds*, the latter of which received first place in the Embers Press Poetry Contest. His collection of poetry *Green Web* received the Contemporary Poetry Series Award and was published by the University of Georgia Press. *El Campo* was published by Capra Press, and *A Rush of Hands* is in its second printing with the University of Arizona Press. He holds an M.F.A. from the University of California at Irvine, where he was also a Regent's Fellow. He is a professor of English and director of the M.F.A. program in creative writing at California State University, San Bernardino.

Photo by Steve Beswick.

Inlandia Institute

Inlandia Institute is a lively center of literary activity located in Riverside, California. It grew out of the highly acclaimed anthology *Inlandia: A Literary Journey through California's Inland Empire,* published by Heyday Books in 2006.

Inlandia Institute strives to nurture the rich and ongoing literary traditions of inland Southern California. Its mission is to recognize, support, and expand literary activity in the Inland Empire by publishing books and sponsoring programs that deepen people's awareness, understanding, and appreciation of this unique, complex, and creatively vibrant area.

For more information about Inlandia Institute titles and programs
please visit www.heydaybooks.com/book_category/inlandia or www.inlandiainstitute.net.

HEYDAY
into California

About Heyday

Heyday is an independent, nonprofit publisher and unique cultural institution. We promote widespread awareness and celebration of California's many cultures, landscapes, and boundary-breaking ideas. Through our well-crafted books, public events, and innovative outreach programs we are building a vibrant community of readers, writers, and thinkers.

Thank You

It takes the collective effort of many to create a thriving literary culture. We are thankful to all the thoughtful people we have the privilege to engage with. Cheers to our writers, artists, editors, storytellers, designers, printers, bookstores, critics, cultural organizations, readers, and book lovers everywhere!

We are especially grateful for the generous funding we've received for our publications and programs during the past year from foundations and hundreds of individual donors. Major supporters include:

Anonymous (3); Acorn Naturalists; Alliance for California Traditional Arts; Arkay Foundation; Judy Avery; James J. Baechle; Paul Bancroft III; BayTree Fund; S. D. Bechtel, Jr. Foundation; Barbara Jean and Fred Berensmeier; Berkeley Civic Arts Program and Civic Arts Commission; Joan Berman; Buena Vista Rancheria/Jesse Flyingcloud Pope Foundation; Lewis and Sheana Butler; California Civil Liberties Public Education Program; Cal Humanities; California Indian Heritage Center Foundation; California State Library; California State Parks Foundation; Keith Campbell Foundation; Candelaria Fund; John and Nancy Cassidy Family Foundation, through Silicon Valley Community Foundation; The Center for California Studies; Graham Chisholm; The Christensen Fund; Jon Christensen; Community Futures Collective; Compton Foundation; Creative Work Fund; Lawrence Crooks; Nik Dehejia; Frances Dinkelspiel and Gary Wayne; The Durfee Foundation; Troy Duster; Earth Island Institute; Eaton Kenyon Fund of the Sacramento Region Community Foundation; Euclid Fund at the East Bay Community Foundation; Foothill Resources, Ltd.; Furthur Foundation; The Fred Gellert Family Foundation; Fulfillco; The Wallace Alexander Gerbode Foundation; Nicola W. Gordon; Wanda Lee Graves and Stephen Duscha; David Guy; The Walter and Elise Haas Fund; Coke and James Hallowell; Historic Resources Group; Sandra and Charles Hobson; G. Scott Hong Charitable Trust; Donna Ewald Huggins; Humboldt Area Foundation; James Irvine Foundation;

Claudia Jurmain; Kendeda Fund; Marty and Pamela Krasney; Guy Lampard and Suzanne Badenhoop; Christine Leefeldt, in celebration of Ernest Callenbach and Malcolm Margolin's friendship; LEF Foundation; Thomas Lockard; Thomas J. Long Foundation; Judith and Brad Lowry-Croul; Kermit Lynch Wine Merchant; Michael McCone; Nion McEvoy and Leslie Berriman; Michael Mitrani; Moore Family Foundation; Michael J. Moratto, in memory of Ernest L. Cassel; Richard Nagler; National Endowment for the Arts; National Wildlife Federation; Native Cultures Fund; The Nature Conservancy; Nightingale Family Foundation; Northern California Water Association; Pacific Legacy, Inc.; The David and Lucile Packard Foundation; Patagonia, Inc.; PhotoWings; Robin Ridder; Alan Rosenus; The San Francisco Foundation; San Manuel Band of Mission Indians; Greg Sarris; Savory Thymes; Sonoma Land Trust; Stone Soup Fresno; Roselyne Chroman Swig; Swinerton Family Fund; Thendara Foundation; Sedge Thomson and Sylvia Brownrigg; TomKat Charitable Trust; Lisa Van Cleef and Mark Gunson; Patricia Wakida; Whole Systems Foundation; Wild by Nature, Inc.; John Wiley & Sons, Inc.; Peter Booth Wiley and Valerie Barth; Bobby Winston; Dean Witter Foundation; The Work-in-Progress Fund of Tides Foundation; and Yocha Dehe Community Fund.

Board of Directors

Getting Involved

To learn more about our publications, events, membership club, and other ways you can participate, please visit www.heydaybooks.com.